Amazon Alexa

———— ✂❧✂❧ ————

Amazon Alexa ultimate user guide for Amazon Echo, Amazon Echo Dot, and Amazon Tap!

Table of Contents

Introduction

Thank you for taking the time to pick up this book about Amazon Alexa.

Amazon Alexa is incredible technology produced by Amazon, that works through the Amazon Echo, Echo Dot, and Amazon Tap devices.

Alexa is Amazon's voice-based assistant, and she will do her best to answer your questions and perform the commands you instruct. People currently use Alexa for a wide variety of things, such as playing music, answering random questions, booking an Uber, ordering Pizza, and even controlling their homes lighting and temperature – though the many uses and capabilities of Alexa are rapidly expanding!

This book serves as a user guide to the Alexa system, regardless of whether you're using an Amazon Echo, Echo Dot, or Amazon Tap. It will take you step by step through the setup of your Alexa device, and describe in detail all of the different features it offers and how to use them.

You will soon discover how to use Alexa for a huge variety of tasks, including how to use Alexa to transform your home into a smart home!

Introduction

Included for your benefit are also the most frequently asked questions that people ask when trying to use their Alexa enabled device. For a bit of fun, there is also a section on the funniest and most entertaining things to ask Alexa.

Once again, thanks for choosing this complete guide to using Amazon Alexa. I hope that it helps you to setup your Alexa device fast, and teaches you all that you want to know about Alexa's amazing features. Enjoy!

Chapter 1:

Overview of Alexa

What Is Amazon Alexa?

A mazon Alexa is Amazon's voice based assistant. Speak your wishes to Alexa, and she'll do her best to fulfill them. She can answer your questions, play you some music, or even order you an Uber.

Once you get used to having Alexa fulfilling your wishes you'll wonder how you ever lived without her. So how can you get started? First, you'll need to get one of Amazon's Alexa enabled devices: The Amazon Echo, Amazon Echo Dot, or Amazon Tap.

Which Alexa enabled device is right for me?

Amazon Echo: This is Amazon's original Alexa enabled device, and also the most expensive option. This Bluetooth speaker features 360° audio, and has 7 microphones so Alexa can hear you even in noisy environments or with music playing. If you don't already have a sound system in your house or you're looking to upgrade, then this is the solution for you. To make the most of the 360° audio, place your Echo in a central location – we think it's a great solution for a busy living room or noisy kitchen. The sound quality is fantastic for the price, and while this is the largest of the Alexa enabled devices the Echo is still quite sleek and unobtrusive. It is currently available in both black and white, but decorative decals are available to transform the Echo to match any décor.

Amazon Echo Dot: At roughly the size of a hocky puck, the Echo Dot is the smallest and cheapest option to get started with Alexa. It has a similar aesthetic to the Echo, and comes in both black and white with decals available for personalisation. Like the Echo, the Echo Dot features 7 microphones so Alexa can hear you no matter where you are in the room. It has a small built-in speaker so Alexa can talk to you, but you'll need to plug in some speakers if you want to use the Echo Dot to play music. This is a great option if you already have an audio setup you love, but want to add Alexa's functionality to it. It's also a fantastic option if you want to be able to talk to Alexa from any room of your house.

If having a smart house is your goal, you could connect many Amazon Echo and Echo Dot devices up in your house. Because Alexa is a smart personal assistant, she'll only respond on the closest device. You could have an Amazon Echo in your living room, and an Echo Dot in your bedrooms so you could talk to Alexa from anywhere! The Echo Dot can be purchased as a single device, or you can also purchase packs of 6 or 12 devices for a discounted price.

Amazon Tap: The Amazon Tap is like a smaller, more portable version of the Amazon Echo. It still has 360° audio and 7 microphones, but it's wireless and runs off battery power. The battery charge should last for up to 9 hours when streaming audio, or up to 3 weeks in standby mode. To charge it, simply set it in the included charging cradle – you should have a full charge again in less than 4 hours.

The downside to the Tap is that unlike the Echo and Echo Dot, Alexa isn't "always-on". You'll need to press a button on the Tap each time you wish to talk to Alexa, which can limit how useful it is. The Tap is a great option if you're looking for a portable Bluetooth speaker, but if you really want to make full use of Alexa then this shouldn't be your first choice.

Pressing a button each time you want to talk to Alexa can be frustrating, and without an Internet connection the Tap will function only as a regular Bluetooth speaker and you won't be able to talk to Alexa. This isn't a problem if you want to use the Tap somewhere you can access Wi-Fi or if you don't mind using a portable hotspot, but if you're primarily using the Tap somewhere with no Internet access then you're paying money for Alexa features you won't be able to use. Think of the Tap as primarily a portable speaker and secondarily as an Alexa enabled device, and you won't be disappointed. The Tap is currently only available in the US.

So how does Alexa work?

The "brains" of Alexa aren't actually in your device, they're stored online in the cloud. When you give Alexa a command or ask her a question, Alexa records your voice and sends your request online to Amazon's "Alexa Voice Services". Amazon uses voice recognition to determine what you've said to Alexa, and then analyses your query to work out what Alexa should do. Amazon then sends a response back to your device with the answer to your request. For example, if you asked Alexa "What is the weather like in New York today?" here's what would happen:

- A recording of your question would be sent online to Amazon

- Voice recognition would determine what you've said and convert it to text

- Natural language processing would be used to determine the meaning of your question

- Amazon finds the current weather forecast for New York

- A response is sent back to your device and Alexa tells you the forecast

All of this should happen seamlessly and in the space of a few seconds as if you were having a regular conversation with a person. We'll cover some basic commands and good questions to ask Alexa in chapter 3.

You may be wondering how Alexa knows when you're talking to her. The Amazon Echo and Echo Dot are always listening for you to give Alexa a command. They'll know you're talking to her if you say the "wake-word". By default, this is "Alexa", but you can change the wake-word to "Echo" or "Amazon" if you prefer. The Amazon Tap doesn't have the same "always-on" capability and will only start recording once you press the talk button on your Tap.

You may be worried that everything you say is being recorded by your Echo or Echo Dot and sent to Amazon. This is not the case. Even though they are always listening, your Echo or Echo Dot will only start sending data to Amazon when they hear the wake-word. If you don't want your Echo or Echo Dot to continually listen for the wake-word, you can temporarily mute your microphones. If you do this, you'll need to unmute your device to be able to talk to Alexa.

Some of the commands you say to Alexa are recorded and stored on your device. This is not designed to track what you're asking Alexa, but is there to improve Alexa's recognition of your voice and speech patterns and make her more accurate. If you have privacy concerns, we'll cover how to mute your devices and delete any recordings later on in the book.

Chapter 2:

Setting up your device

In this chapter we will cover how to setup your Alexa enabled device so that it's ready to use!

To setup Alexa you will need:

- A Wi-Fi connection

- An Echo, Echo Dot, or Tap

- A phone or tablet running Fire OS 3.0 or higher, Android 4.4 or higher, or iOS 8.0 or higher OR a Wi-Fi enabled computer

Step One: Download the Alexa app

Download the Alexa app from the Apple app store, Google Play or the Amazon app store. Once the app has finished downloading, please sign in to your Amazon account.

If you are using a computer to setup Alexa, browse to https://alexa.amazon.com on your computer using Safari, Chrome, Firefox, Microsoft Edge, or Internet Explorer, and then login to your Amazon account.

Step Two: Power on your device

Plug in your device and turn it on. The light ring on your device should turn blue and then orange, and then Alexa will greet you. Your device is now in setup mode.

Step Three: Connect your device to Wi-Fi.

- In the Alexa app or on your computer, open the navigation panel on the left side of the screen and select "Settings" then "Set up a new device".

- Press and hold the Action button (Echo/Echo Dot) or Wi-Fi/Bluetooth button (Tap) on your device until the light ring turns orange. A list of Wi-Fi networks should now appear in the Alexa app.

- Select your Wi-Fi network and enter your password. If you are planning on setting up more than one Alexa device on your network, select the option to "Save your Wi-Fi password to Amazon". This will make setup faster on your other devices.

- Select "Connect" and your device will now connect to the Wi-Fi network.

Step Four: Voice Training

This step is optional, but it will improve Alexa's voice recognition accuracy. Within the Alexa app select "Settings" and then "Voice Training". Alexa will now have you repeat some phrases to improve her voice recognition. Ideally, you should repeat this process with everyone who will be using Alexa so that she becomes familiar with their voices.

Step Five: Customize your Alexa experience

Now is a good opportunity to add some details to your Alexa app to customize your experience. At the very least, you should set your device location so that time and weather information are accurate and Alexa can find local business information.

To set the device location:

- In the Alexa app, open the left navigation panel, and then select "Settings".

- Select your device.

- In the Device location section, select "Edit".

- Enter the complete address, including the street name, city, state, and ZIP code.

- Select "Save".

Other details you may want to add are your preferred news sources, favorite sports teams, commute details, and Google calendar accounts. You can change these settings by selecting "Settings" and then "Account" within the Alexa app. These details are used to provide you with customized answers when asking Alexa for the news, sports scores, and traffic conditions, or when adding items to your calendar or to-do list.

Chapter 3:

Basic Commands

Now that your device is set up you can start giving Alexa some commands. Alexa has a variety of built in commands, and you can add more functionality by adding "Skills" to Alexa. For now, we're just going to cover the basics, and will talk more about adding skills later in the book. Some of the following commands require you to have customized your Alexa experience by setting your device location, commute, sports and news preferences, and linking a Google Calendar.

Universal Commands

"Alexa, help" – Alexa provides help

"Alexa, repeat" – Alexa will repeat what she last said

"Alexa, stop" – Alexa will stop the current activity, e.g. music playback

"Alexa, cancel" – Cancels the previous command

Chapter 3: Basic Commands

Volume Commands

"Alexa, mute" – mutes Alexa

"Alexa, unmute" – Unmutes Alexa

"Alexa, set volume to [0-10]" – Sets volume

"Alexa, louder" – Increases volume

"Alexa, turn up/down the volume" – Increases/decreases volume

"Alexa, turn up the bass" – Increases the bass

"Alexa, turn down the treble" – Decreases the treble

"Alexa, increase the midrange" – Increases the midrange

Time and date

"Alexa, set an alarm for [time]." – Sets an alarm

"Alexa, wake me up at [time] in the morning." – Sets an alarm

"Alexa, set a repeating alarm for [day] at [time]." – Sets a repeating alarm

"Alexa, when's my next alarm?" – Alexa will tell you when you next alarm is

"Alexa, cancel my alarm for 2 p.m." – Cancels alarm

"Alexa, snooze." – Snoozes alarm

"Alexa, set a timer for [##] minutes." – Sets a timer

"Alexa, how much time is left on my timer?" – Alexa returns how long is left on your timer

"Alexa, what time is it?" – Alexa tells the current time

"Alexa, what's the date?" – Alexa tells the current date

"Alexa, when is [holiday] this year?" – Alexa tells you when the holiday is

Math

"Alexa, how many [units] are in [units]?" – Converts between units

"Alexa, what's [number] plus [number]?" – Alexa can add, subtract, multiply and divide

"Alexa, [#] factorial." – Alexa can do advanced math like factorials

Dictionary

"Alexa, what's the definition of [word]?" – Alexa tells you the word definition

"Alexa, how do you spell [word]?" – Alexa tells you how to spell a word

To do/Shopping lists

"Alexa, add [task] to my to-do list" – Adds the task to your to-do list

"Alexa, add [item] to my shopping list" – Adds an item to your shopping list

Chapter 3: Basic Commands

"Alexa, what's on my to-do/shopping list" – Alexa tells you what's on your list

"Alexa, add [event] to my calendar for [day] at [time]" - Adds an event to your calendar

"Alexa, what's on for today" – Checks your calendar for today

"Alexa, what's my mission" – Checks your calendar

News and weather

"Alexa, what's in the news?" – Checks your news headlines

"Alexa, what's the weather like?" – Checks the weather forecast

"Alexa, what's the weather going to be like on [day]? – Checks the weather forecast for a given day

"Alexa, what's traffic like?" – Gets traffic updates

"Alexa, did the [team] win?" – Gets sport results

"Alexa, what's my Flash Briefing?" – Alexa will give you your flash briefing from the news sources you follow

"Alexa, give me my Sports Update." – Updates you on your preferred sports teams

Media

"Alexa, play some music." – Starts music playback with the default music service

"Alexa, play music by [artist]." – Plays songs by the specified artist

"Alexa, what's playing?" – Tells you what's currently playing

"Alexa, play" – Starts music playback

"Alexa, next." – Skips to the next song

"Alexa, restart." – Restarts a song

"Alexa, loop" – Loops the current song

"Alexa, stop playing in [##] minutes." – Alexa will stop playback after the specified number of minutes

"Alexa, play [title] on Audible – Plays an audiobook from Audible

"Alexa, resume my book." – Resumes last played audio book

"Alexa, next chapter" – Skips to the next chapter in an audio book

"Alexa, previous chapter." – Goes to the previous audiobook chapter

"Alexa, read me my Kindle book." – Alexa reads your kindle book to you

Amazon

"Alexa, reorder [item]." – Reorders a previously purchased item

"Alexa, track my order." – Tracks your Amazon orders

"Alexa, order an Echo," – Orders an Amazon Echo

"Alexa, add [item] to my cart." – Adds an item to your Amazon cart

"Alexa, what are your deals?" – Finds current Amazon deals

Local information

"Alexa, what movies are playing?" – Finds movies playing nearby

"Alexa, what action movies are playing tonight?" – Finds action movies playing nearby at the specified time

"Alexa, find me a nearby pizza restaurant." – Finds local businesses

"Alexa, find the address for [local business]" – Alexa can find addresses, phone numbers and operating hours

General Questions

"Alexa, Wikipedia: [subject]." – Alexa reads the first paragraph of the specified Wikipedia article

"Alexa, tell me more." – Alexa will continue reading the Wikipedia article

"Alexa, [general question] – Alexa can find the answer to most general questions

Chapter 4:

Adding More Skills to Alexa

Have you got the hang of using some basic commands with Alexa? Do you want to add some more features?

Adding more features to Alexa is easy. Features within Alexa are called "Skills". You can think of a skill as an app that Alexa can run. There are lots of different skills that have been created by third party developers to add functionality to Alexa, and best of all they're free to enable on Alexa!

There are a few different ways you can add skills to Alexa. If you already know the exact name of the skill you would like to add you could say "Alexa, enable [skill name] skill". Please note that if a skill requires you to link an account such as with Fitbit or Uber you won't be able to enable it by voice.

If you don't know the exact name of a skill you would like to add or you need to link an account, you can use the Alexa app or the Alexa skills store on Amazon to add a skill.

Chapter 4: Adding More Skills to Alexa

To enable a skill in the Alexa app:

- From the left navigation panel, select "Skills".

- Use the search bar to enter keywords or select "Categories" to browse through skill categories.

- When you see a skill you want to use, select "Enable Skill".

To enable a skill using the Alexa skills store:

- Browse to https://www.amazon.com/skills on your computer

- Use the search bar to enter keywords or select a category on the left side of the screen to browse through skill categories.

- Select a skill you'd like to enable

- Click "Enable Skill"

To use a skill you've enabled within Alexa, you need to use the skill invocation name. For example, you could say "Alexa, open Uber" or "Alexa, ask Uber to request a ride" to use the Uber skill. In this case "Uber" is the skill invocation name. The invocation name for each skill is unique, and it's not always the same as the skill name itself. It can get confusing to remember a lot of skill invocation names, but if you forget the invocation name for a skill, then you can look up the skill details again using the Alexa app.

If you ever need help with a skill or aren't sure what commands you can use, you can say, "Alexa, help with [skill name] and Alexa will give you some assistance. You can also look at the skill details within the Alexa app for information.

If you no longer wish to use a particular Alexa skill, you can disable it by saying "Alexa, disable [skill name] skill" or you can disable it within the Alexa app by doing the following:

- From the left navigation panel, select "Skills".

- Use the search bar to find the skill you wish to disable

- When you find the skill you want to disable, select "Disable Skill".

Chapter 5:

Recommended Skills

The Alexa app store is growing fast with over 4,000 awesome skills that can be activated using your voice with Alexa enabled devices!

In the previous chapter, we covered how to add these skills to your Alexa device. In this chapter we will be giving you some recommendations for the best, most useful, and also funny skills that you'll want to consider enabling.

Here are our top suggestions that you might want to check out in the Alexa Skills store.

Fitbit

If you own and use a Fitbit, you'll be happy to hear that it can now integrate with Alexa on all Alexa enabled devices!

This allows you to get fast updates on a variety of different stats, such as steps taken, exercise goals, and sleep information.

The downsides are that it doesn't work with multiple Fitbit accounts, and is still quite basic in its functions.

7-Minute Workout

Another exercise skill, the 7-Minute workout allows you to try a variety of different short workouts, and track your progress as you do so!

This skill allows you to perform a quick, 7-minute, fat-burning workout with the help of your Echo, Echo Dot, or Amazon Tap. Even better, you can perform the workout whilst wearing a Fitbit to have even more data recorded by Alexa!

Stock Exchange

The Stock Exchange skill allows you to keep an eye on the performance of your portfolio, as well as gather information about the market.

Currently, Alexa can provide you information about a range of stocks. Unfortunately, Alexa often misunderstands you with this skill when asking about certain stocks, and subsequently provides the wrong information.

CryptoCurrency

This skill lets you instantly check the prices of Bitcoin. If you trade Bitcoin, this simple skill can be handy for tracking the market value more quickly than before.

Capital One

The Capital One skill allows you to check your bank transactions, balance, and pay bills, all using voice commands.

This is a very useful skill, though you do need to be cautious of the obvious security threats that using this may pose.

Mortgage Calculator

This skill may sound boring, but it's very practical. It allows you to calculate monthly payments based on your principal amount, loan length, and interest rate.

Yo Momma Jokes

A silly skill, Yo Momma Jokes will tell you a whole heap of different jokes that will appeal to most. However, it doesn't have an age setting and so some of the jokes might not be suitable for the whole family!

4A Fart

Possibly the silliest skill in the store is the 4A Fart skill. As you might have guessed, this skill allows Alexa to make fart noises on command. Simple, but funny.

Pickup Lines

A funny skill for the guys to use, Pickup Lines will cause Alexa to fire off some dirty one-liners. Not only that, she also interjects in-between pickup lines with some funny comments, giving her more personality than you'll see in almost all other skills.

SmartThings

If you want to create a smart home, then the SmartThings skill is what you're looking for. This allows Alexa to perform a range of functions within your home, such as controlling lights, thermostats, and security systems.

However, this skill does require that you also purchase a SmartThings hub, and some of the equipment such as lights and security components can be quite expensive.

Mosaic

Mosaic is a skill that allows you to control your Hue lights, Nest Learning Thermostat, and even your Tesla car! It allows you to perform functions such as dimming lights, and changing the temperature of your house.

The downside however is that the required components such as compatible lights and thermostat will come at an additional cost.

Automatic

The Automatic skill lets you sync Alexa with your car. It can provide information such as car location, gas, and the distance you have driven!

It does however require an Automatic account and adapter, which will come at an additional cost.

The Magic Door

A great skill for children, The Magic Door allows you to create your own story. Using the skill, you can choose up to three different story settings, and each choice you make will alter the outcome of the tale. It takes story telling to a whole new place, making it an interactive activity.

Right now however, the stories are quite short and there are only a limited number available. As time goes on though, you should expect more to be added.

Akinator

The Akinator skill is essentially Alexa's version of '20 questions'.

You simply think of an object, and Alexa will begin questioning you to find out what it is. Make sure to answer clear though, otherwise the skill won't work to its full potential.

Amazing Word Master Game

This skill is one of the best games for Alexa so far!

Alexa starts by saying a word, to which you have to respond with a word that begins with the letter that Alexa's ended with.

This continues on and on, and you receive points based on the length of the words you say. The game goes on until someone fails to respond, or you choose to end the game.

Overall, it's a fun and mentally stimulating game to play on your own, or with friends.

The Wayne Investigation

This skill is a fun, Batman adventure game.

Similar to The Magic Door skill, you get to interact with the story and make choices along the way. This one is Batman themed, and has a variety of different stories and options to choose from.

The audio is really high quality, and this is easily one of the best game skills currently available!

Chapter 5: Recommended Skills

Jeopardy

Just like the TV show, the Jeopardy skill will fire off questions for you to answer. This helps you to build your general knowledge, and can be a fun way to challenge friends!

Trainer Tips

For the Pokemon lovers out there, Trainer Tips will help you to increase your Pokémon knowledge! This skill can spout out random Pokémon facts, and also answer specific questions about the Pokémon you want to learn about.

Potterhead Quiz

The Potterhead Quiz is a simple skill that will fire off questions about the world of Harry Potter. Test your Potter knowledge against your friends with this fun skill.

TV Shows

TV Shows allows you to ask Alexa when your favorite shows are playing. Be sure to be clear with your commands though, as this skill can sometimes get mixed up between different shows if you don't speak clearly!

Uber

The Uber skill works similarly to the app, and lets you request an Uber using your voice. It can also provide you information on the ride options and status, and can even be used to cancel the Uber.

Lyft

Uber's main competitor, Lyft, also has a skill available. It works in the same way, allowing you to order a Lyft using a simple voice command.

In addition, you can enquire about Lyft's pricing by asking things like "Alexa, ask Lyft how much a Lyft Plus will cost from home to work".

1-800-Flowers

This skill makes gift giving easy, and allows you to send flowers through a simple voice command!

You can choose from a variety of floral arrangements, and set a delivery date of your choice. Prior to using this skill, you will need to create a 1-800 Flowers account, and then sync it up.

The only real negative to this skill is that it currently doesn't have as wide of a selection as you can get from the online version.

WineMate

The WineMate skill helps you to choose the perfect wine to pair with your food. Simply enable the skill, and then ask Alexa what wine would go well with (XYZ) food! It works in the opposite way too, meaning you can ask Alexa which food would go well with your chosen wine.

What Beer

Just like the WineMate skill, What Beer helps you to choose which beer you should have with your meal.

Chapter 5: Recommended Skills

The Bartender

The Bartender is a fun skill that provides you with recipes for your favorite cocktails! In an instant, Alexa will tell you the different ingredients you need for your desired cocktail, and will even give you drink suggestions.

Campbell's Kitchen

The Campbell's Kitchen skill is an extension of the well-known recipe app of the same name.

In an instant, Alexa will be able to give you recipes for a huge selection of meals. It can also be used to send you an e-mail or app summary showing the recipes you've chosen.

QuickBits

Another food skill, QuickBits is designed for those who don't have much time to spend in the kitchen. This skill provides you with a ton of different recipes that can all be made in 10-minutes or less!

All you have to do is ask QuickBits how to make your favorite fast meal, and Alexa will respond with the recipe!

Meat Thermometer

Another food-related skill, Meat Thermometer tells you the correct internal temperature you should bring your meat to when cooking. It has information on a range of different meats, and is a simple way to improve your cooking!

Food Finder

This cool skill will let you know where you can find food in your area. Simply tell the skill "I want Thai food in (insert zip code)" and it will let you know the available places!

It works with all different food types, and saves you searching through web results to find a suitable place.

Domino's Pizza

A simple but awesome skill, this allows you to be even lazier when ordering pizza. Now you don't even need to move, and can order from Dominos with just a voice command!

You can also track your order status with this skill, and it even remembers your recent orders, and your favorites list. This one is currently only available in the US, but it's likely it will become available elsewhere soon!

Kayak

Kayak is a great travel skill that helps you to research prices for future trips. Simply ask Alexa where you can travel to for '$X', or enquire about flight prices for certain dates.

Kayak will search the web, and give you the different price options for trips instantly.

Guitar Tuner

If you're a guitar player, you definitely want to download this skill!

It simply plays the guitar notes from the low E string, up to the high E string, so you can tune your guitar by ear.

Chapter 5: Recommended Skills

HuffPost

The HuffPost skill will read out the headlines from the Huffington Post so that you can get a quick idea of what's happening in the news, and what you might like to read about.

1 Minute Mindfulness

This skill lets you enter a 1-minute sound meditation. If you're feeling stressed out and need a quick break, you can enable this skill to begin meditating right away.

You can select different styles of meditation too, such as a forest meditation, or a beach meditation.

Twitter

The official Twitter skill will read out tweets from your timeline, find trending topics, and read out tweets that you have liked in the past.

If you don't want to pick up your phone to find out what's been said recently on Twitter, then just say "Alexa, ask Twitter what's happening".

Ask My Buddy

This skill is great for people with disabilities, as it allows you to send a distress signal to friends and family. If you need help, or in the case of an accident or emergency, you can use this skill to send distress messages to one, or all, of your chosen contacts.

Chapter 6:

Smart Home

One of the biggest draw cards for Alexa is the ability to use it to control your smart home. If you've already started to make your home smart, you'll be happy to know that Alexa is compatible with a large number of devices, and there are already skills available in the Alexa Skills Store to make it simple to get everything connected.

If you haven't already purchased any smart devices, now is a great time to start. You can get some fantastic deals by shopping for devices in the Alexa smart home store, and as a bonus you'll know that all of your devices are Alexa compatible.

Device Recommendations

Here are a few of our favorite Alexa compatible smart devices. Most of the devices on our recommendation list are beginner friendly and are easy to get set up with Alexa. The most important thing is to choose devices that you will use. There's no point in having a great device if it doesn't suit your needs!

Lighting

Smart lighting is a really popular place to start when making your home smart, and there are a lot of different lighting solutions available. Our recommendations here are just for basic indoor lighting, but don't be fooled by this list. There are plenty of different lighting types and specialty lighting solutions out there if you want to do something special.

Philips Hue White Starter Kit

This is the cheapest way to get started with Phillips Hue lights in Alexa. This kit comes with 2 soft, white LED lights, and also a Hue Hub. A Hue Hub is necessary to connect Hue lights to Alexa, and each hub can connect up to 50 lights so you can keep adding lights as you make your home smarter. The lights included in this kit are probably the most basic lights in the Phillips Hue range, but if all you want to be able to do is turn your lights off and on they are perfect. We're a fan of Phillips Hue lights because they have a huge range of lighting and are easy to set up.

Phillips Hue White Ambience Starter Kit

This kit is similar to the Phillips Hue White Starter kit, but the included lights have some additional features. The two lights in this kit can be adjusted to various different shades of white light, so you can adjust the lighting to suit your mood. Also included is a Hue Hub and a wireless light dimmer switch, which is a nice touch if some members of your household would still like to be able to manually adjust the lights.

Philips Hue White and Color Starter Kit

This is Phillips' best selling Hue starter kit for a reason. This kit is pricier than our other recommended Hue starter kits, but it allows you to play with colored lighting. This kit includes 3 color LED lights, and a Hue Hub. Alexa currently has limited support for colored Hue lights, but this is likely to change in the near future. For now, you are able to turn lights on and off with Alexa or display programmed light themes.

Lifx Color 1000 LED light

If you don't want to wait for Phillips to add increased support for their colored lights, this is the best option to buy right now. Lifx lights are expensive but they have full compatibility with Alexa and you don't need a hub to get them connected.

Lifx White 800 LED

Not sure if you'll like having a smart home? If you just want to test things out, then this is the bulb to buy. Because Lifx lights don't need a hub to get connected to Alexa, you can just buy a single bulb rather than needing to buy a starter kit like you do with Phillips Hue. This bulb is a color adjustable white light, so you can adjust your lighting to fit your mood.

Outlets and Plugs

Want to make a dumb appliance smart? The easiest way to do this is to use a smart outlet that will power up your appliance on demand. Our recommendations here are for outlets that don't require a smart home hub to connect to Alexa. There are many more options if you use a smart home hub to connect to Alexa, but this is an extra cost you may not want to spend when you're first getting started.

Outlets connected via a hub have the advantage of being able to be smaller, and you can even find a few options that will allow you to replace your existing wall outlets with smart outlets for a sleek, seamless look. All of our recommendations below are for quite bulky plugs, so please be aware that these may block access to other outlets.

Belkin WeMo Switch & Belkin WeMo Insight Switch

These smart plugs both connect directly to your Wi-Fi so there is no need for a smart home hub to connect to Alexa. The WeMo Insight Switch is the pricier option of the two, but it adds the ability to track electricity usage. The downside to these plugs is that if you ever have a power outage, you will need to manually turn each plug back on which can be a pain if you have a few of them.

TP-Link HS100 Smart Plug & TP-Link HS110 Smart Plug with Energy Monitoring

These plugs are a less expensive alternative to the WeMo Switches. They offer similar functionality to the WeMo Switches with a more utilitarian look. Smart plugs are bulky because of all the electronics crammed inside them, so it will come down to personal preference which plugs you find suit your home the best.

Thermostats

Support for thermostats is a new feature for Alexa, and all of our recommendations below will work straight out of the box, with no need for a smart home hub. A smart thermostat is a great feature for a smart home as it can save you hundreds of dollars by automatically adjusting your heating and cooling, turning it off when no one is home. A smart thermostat may be a pricy investment, but it will pay for itself with the savings on your electricity bill.

Nest Learning Thermostat

This is an Amazon best seller and it's no surprise why. It's a modern and sleek looking device and it boasts an impressive list of features. If you're looking to save money on your electricity bill, the Home/Away Assist and energy usage features are particularly helpful. The Nest Learning thermostat is the most expensive thermostat on our recommendation list but we think it's worth it for the beautiful design and potential to save you money on your electricity bills.

Ecobee3 Thermostat with Sensor

The Ecobee3 thermostat is a great option if you have a large house to heat or cool. What sets this thermostat apart from other options is the ability to add extra sensors. Ecobee3 sensors detect temperature and room occupancy, so that the Ecobee3 can address problems such as hot or cold spots in rooms. If you've ever had a problem with some rooms in your house being too hot or too cold while the room with the thermostat is the perfect temperature, the Ecobee3 aims to solve that by averaging the temperature out over your whole house to ensure maximum comfort. This set comes with one extra sensor, but additional sensors are available for purchase and the Ecobee3 can support up to 32 of them.

Sensi Smart Thermostat

The Sensi Smart Thermostat boasts that no other thermostat works in more homes. It has a very easy install process, and you can be up and running in under 15-minutes. The design of the Sensi Smart Thermostat is similar to that of a traditional thermostat, and there are still physical buttons to adjust temperature settings. It would be a good option if not everyone in your home is onboard with the idea of a smart home, or you do not like the sleek button-less aesthetic of the Nest or Ecobee3 thermostats.

Smart Home Hubs

A smart home hub connects all of your smart devices together. A hub can be useful to act as a middleman to integrate with smart devices that aren't Wi-Fi enabled, but it's not a necessity to get started with making your home smart. More and more devices are coming on to the market that directly support connecting to Wi-Fi, so you'll only need a hub if you want to use devices that aren't Wi-Fi enabled. Not every smart device will work with every hub, so take your time to consider which features you would like in your smart home and research which devices are compatible with each other.

Samsung SmartThings Hub

The Samsung SmartThings Hub boasts compatibility with a wide range of devices including some third party devices. The SmartThings platform is open, meaning that any manufacturer can choose to make SmartThings compatible devices. This gives you a great deal of choice and a wide range of devices to choose from. The SmartThings hub would be a particularly good choice if you own Samsung appliances such as fridges, ovens, washers, or dryers with SmartThings compatibility.

Wink Hub 2

For a long time, Samsung were leading in terms of number of compatible devices, but the newly released Wink Hub 2 is putting Wink ahead of the pack. Wink already had great reviews on their original Wink Hub, and now they've followed up on that success by adding compatibility for even more wireless protocols. Unless you already have SmartThings enabled Samsung appliances, it's worth spending the extra money to get the Wink Hub 2 instead. If the extra features in the Wink Hub 2 don't appeal to you, take advantage of retailers selling out old stock of the original Wink Hub and get yourself a bargain.

ISY994Zw Series

If you've been into home automation for a long time and still have some older X10 devices, then this is the hub for you. It's an expensive solution, but this hub allows you to integrate both your older X10 devices and newer Insteon and Z-Wave compatible devices. It's a great solution if you're looking to slowly replace your X10 devices as they become obsolete. It has a steeper learning curve than the other recommendations in this list, but it offers far more options if you're someone who likes to tinker.

Getting set up

So how do you get your smart devices set up with Alexa? For most devices this should be simple. Firstly, follow the instructions that came with your smart device to get it set up on your Wi-Fi network. Setup will vary depending on your device – contact the device manufacturer if you're unsure of what to do.

Chapter 6: Smart Home

Once your device is connected to your Wi-Fi, you're ready to connect it to Alexa by installing the relevant skill. You can find home automation skills by doing the following:

- In the Alexa app select the "**Menu**" icon (this looks like 3 horizontal lines)

- Select "**Smart Home**".

- Select "**Get More Smart Home Skills**".

- Browse or search keywords for the skill for your smart home device and select "**Enable Skill**".

- If prompted, sign in with your third-party information and then follow the prompts to complete setup.

Not all smart devices will need a skill to allow them to be discovered. These include some Phillips Hue and Belkin WeMo devices. To connect these devices just say "Alexa, discover devices".

Once you have your skills installed and your devices have been discovered, you can do some further setup by organizing your devices into groups. Devices that have been sorted into groups can be controlled as a group so you can give a simple command to Alexa such as "Alexa, turn on bedroom lights" to turn on all of your bedroom lights.

To create a smart home device group:

- In the Alexa app, open the left navigation panel and select "**Smart Home**".

- Under "**Groups**", select "**Create group**".

- Enter the name of the group into the text field.

- Select the devices you want to add to the group, and then click "**Add**".

You are now set up to control your smart devices using Alexa. Here are a few of the commands you can use.

- "Alexa, turn on/off [device/group name]." – Turn on a device or group of devices

- "Alexa, turn on/off [scene]." – Toggle on/off a programmed scene

- "Alexa, set [device/group name] to [##]%." – Set the brightness of compatible lights

- "Alexa, brighten/dim [device/group name]." – Adjust the brightness of compatible lights

- "Alexa, set [thermostat name] temperature to [##] degrees." – Adjust the thermostat

- "Alexa, [Increase/decrease] the [thermostat name] temperature." – Adjust the thermostat

- "Alexa, set my bedroom fan to [##]%." – Change fan speed

- "Alexa, turn on [channel/activity]." – Start an activity

Some smart home skills may require you to use the invocation name when giving Alexa a command. You can find details about your smart home skills and which commands you can use by finding the skill details in the Alexa app.

Chapter 6: Smart Home

__Non Alexa Compatible devices__

So what can you do if you have a smart device that is not Alexa compatible? There's no need to despair, you can still get your device working with Alexa by using If This Then That (IFTTT). IFTTT is a free home automation service that has native support on Amazon Alexa. This means that you can use IFTTT without enabling a new skill.

To get started with IFTTT on Alexa, you will need to create an account at https://ifttt.com/ and then connect your account to Alexa by doing the following:

- On the IFTTT webpage select "**Channels**" in the top right corner

- Select "**Amazon Alexa**"

- Click "**Connect**"

- Enter your Amazon login details

In IFTTT you create what are known as "recipes" to control your devices. To create a recipe:

- On the IFTTT webpage click "My Recipes"

- Click "Create a recipe"

IFTTT recipes consist of a trigger and an action. In our case we want our trigger to be a command in Alexa, and the action will be whatever you want your smart device to do in response. To add Alexa as your recipe trigger:

- Click "**this**" in the recipe form

- Select the "**Amazon Alexa**" channel

- Select "**say a specific phrase**"

- Enter the phrase you'd like to use

- Click "**Create trigger**"

You now need to add an action to the "that" portion of your recipe. This will be the action that you want your smart device to perform. To do this:

- Select "**that**" in the recipe form

- Select the channel for your device (you will need to have authorized this channel)

- Select an action

- Click "**Create action**"

The last thing you need to do is enter a description for your recipe and click on "**Create recipe**".

Now that your recipe has been created you can run it by saying "Alexa, trigger [phrase]" where phrase is the phrase you chose when creating your recipe.

Chapter 7:

The Future of Alexa

So if you've used Alexa for a while now you might be wondering what the future may bring. New skills are being added to the Alexa skills store everyday, and Alexa is constantly being updated to offer new features. The most useful feature that was added to Alexa in 2016 was the ability to ask Alexa a general question and have her answer it using the Bing search engine. This means that Alexa can now answer almost anything.

Amazon is constantly improving Alexa's voice recognition and language processing features. Google Home was recently released in November 2016 and has the functionality to hold a conversation. So you can ask Google Assistant a question, and then ask a second follow up question and Google Assistant will infer your meaning from the context. It's likely that we'll see a similar feature in Alexa soon. How exciting will it be to have a conversation with Alexa and have her intelligently respond!

The other feature we're really excited about is support for a wider range of countries. Alexa was originally only available in the US, and was released in the UK and Germany in October 2016. 2017 should see support added for more markets, and more skills will appear in the UK and German Alexa skill stores.

Chapter 7: The Future of Alexa

Many third party manufacturers are beginning to integrate Alexa into their devices, so you'll no longer be limited to using Alexa on an Echo, Echo Dot, or Tap. Here are a few recently released or upcoming Alexa compatible devices.

Lenovo Smart Assistant

Lenovo Smart Assistant is an alternative to the Amazon Echo and will be released in May 2017. Boasting 8 microphones, 360° audio, and a variety of colors to choose from, the Lenovo Smart Assistant is likely to be a very strong competitor to the Echo. Two versions are due to be released, the base model and the upgraded model. The base model is set to retail for $129USD and the upgraded model with better audio quality is set to retail for $179USD.

Invoxia Triby

Released in April 2016, the Triby was the first non-Amazon Alexa enabled device. Like the Amazon Echo it features a Bluetooth speaker, but in a very different format. The Triby is a small retro looking square box that is designed to be stuck to your fridge like a giant fridge magnet. It has an e-ink screen to take notes on, and adds other features such as the ability to use it as a speakerphone. The biggest downsides noted by reviewers are the poor sound quality and slow response times when asking Alexa a question.

C by GE LED Lamp

The C by GE LED Lamp is a small, modern table lamp set to be released between April and June 2017. GE hasn't released pricing details yet, but it is likely the price will be less than the cost of an Amazon Echo.

LG InstaView smart refrigerator

Yes, soon you will be able to get an Alexa enabled fridge! Alexa has proven to be very helpful in the kitchen with her ability to search for recipes, and LG has decided that adding her to your fridge is a sensible idea. LG haven't given price or availability details yet, but based on previous smart fridges offered by LG, it's unlikely to be cheap.

FABRIQ Smart Speaker

Like the Amazon Tap, the FABRIQ smart speaker is an Alexa enabled portable Bluetooth speaker. The biggest difference between the two is the price. The FABRIQ smart speaker sells for only $49USD, which is a lot less than a Tap for similar functionality. The FABRIQ smart speaker is currently available in three distinctive designs, and has a very unique look. You'll certainly stand out from the crowd with this speaker.

Chapter 8:

50 Fun Things to Ask Alexa

Besides using your Alexa enabled device for practical purposes, you can also have a bit of fun with it too! The following questions and comments will all get a witty response from Alexa that is sure to keep you entertained!

1. Alexa, how old is Santa Claus?

2. Alexa, can I tell you a secret?

3. Alexa, what's the magic word?

4. Alexa, do you smoke?

5. Alexa, are you smoking?

6. Alexa, what is your favorite food?

7. Alexa, what is your favorite drink?

8. Alexa, are you hungry/thirsty?

9. Alexa, what is your feature?

10. Alexa, do you have any pets?

11. Alexa, who is your best friend?

12. Alexa, what religion are you?

13. Alexa, are you God?

14. Alexa, are you evil?

15. Alexa, what language do you speak?

16. Alexa, am I funny?

17. Alexa, can I tell you a joke?

18. Alexa, what is happiness?

19. Alexa, what size shoe do you wear?

20. Alexa, what makes you happy?

21. Alexa, who's on first?

22. Alexa, fire photon torpedos.

23. Alexa, live long and prosper.

24. Alexa, open the pod bay doors.

25. Alexa, these aren't the droids you're looking for.

26. Alexa, take me to your leader.

27. Alexa, does this unit have a soul?

28. Alexa, do you like green eggs and ham?

29. Alexa, one fish, two fish.

30. Alexa, what was the Lorax?

31. Alexa, why do you sit there like that?

32. Alexa, why do birds suddenly appear?

33. Alexa, to be or not to be.

34. Alexa, beam me up.

35. Alexa, I am your father.

36. Alexa, may the force be with you.

37. Alexa, Tea. Earl Grey. Hot.

38. Alexa, Warp 10

39. Alexa, party time!

40. Alexa, are you working?

41. Alexa, heads or tails?

42. Alexa, random number between "x" and "y".

43. Alexa, what number are you thinking of?

44. Alexa, count by ten.

45. Alexa, rock, paper, scissors.

46. Alexa, random fact

47. Alexa, what is the meaning of life?

48. Alexa, when is the end of the world?

49. Alexa, when am I going to die?

50. Alexa, what is the airspeed velocity of an unladen swallow?

Chapter 9:

Troubleshooting and FAQ

I'm concerned for my privacy; how can I stop Alexa from listening to my conversations?

If you have an Echo or Echo Dot you can mute the microphone on your device. The mute button is located on the top of the device, and looks like a microphone with a slash through it. The light ring on your device will glow red when the microphone is muted and you will not be able to wake Alexa with the wake word. To resume using Alexa, unmute your microphone by pressing the mute button again.

I'd like to delete the recordings Alexa has taken of my voice.

Alexa records some of your queries to improve her recognition of your voice. If you delete these recordings, Alexa may not be as accurate at recognizing the questions you ask her. If you still wish to delete these recordings, you can do so by taking the following steps:

1. Open the Alexa app.

2. Select "**Settings**" in the navigation panel of the left

3. Select "**History**".

4. Select a recording from the list

5. Select the **"Play"** icon to listen to the recording if you wish to.

6. Select **"Delete voice recording"**

The light ring is orange and spinning clockwise. What is happening?

Your device is attempting to connect to Wi-Fi. If this happens often it indicates that your device is receiving a weak Wi-Fi signal and may be too far away from your router. You should try moving your device closer to your router. This could also indicate that your network is congested or something is interfering with your Wi-Fi network. To combat this, you can try reducing the number of devices that are connected to your network and moving your device away from potential sources of interference such as microwaves and baby monitors.

If none of the above helps the issue, you can try restarting your device and your router. This will resolve most intermittent Wi-Fi issues.

1. Turn off your router, and then wait 30 seconds. Ask your router manufacturer or Internet service provider if you are unsure how to do this.

2. Turn on your router and then wait for it to restart. You will usually have some status lights to indicate when this process is complete.

3. While your network hardware restarts, unplug the power adapter from your device for three seconds, and then plug it back in.

4. Once your device and router have restarted, attempt to connect to Wi-Fi again.

The light ring is violet and flashing. What is wrong?

This indicates that something went wrong during Wi-Fi setup. The first thing you should do is attempt the Wi-Fi setup again. Make sure you are connecting to the right network and that you are entering your network password if one is required. Ensure that your password and other details are correct.

You should check that other devices such as your laptop or mobile phone are able to connect to the network. If they cannot, this indicates that there is a problem with your network. You may need to contact your Internet service provider for help with troubleshooting network problems.

If you had previously saved your Wi-Fi password within the Alexa app, you may need to update your password within the Alexa app if it has changed recently.

If none of the above helps the issue, you can try restarting your device and your router. This will resolve most intermittent Wi-Fi issues.

1. Turn off your router, and then wait 30 seconds. Ask your router manufacturer or Internet service provider if you are unsure how to do this.

2. Turn on your router and then wait for it to restart. You will usually have some status lights to indicate when this process is complete.

3. While your network hardware restarts, unplug the power adapter from your device for three seconds, and then plug it back in.

4. Once your device and router have restarted, attempt to connect to Wi-Fi again.

As a last resort you may need to contact your router manufacturer or Internet service provider for assistance.

Alexa has trouble understanding me. What can I do?

You can do voice training to improve how well Alexa understands your voice. Within the Alexa app select "Settings" and then "Voice Training". Alexa will now have you repeat some phrases to improve her voice recognition.

If this doesn't resolve the issue, you may need to move your device to a better location. It is recommended that your device is at least 8-inches away from walls or other objects, and it is not placed on the floor. You should also try to reduce the amount of background noise in your environment and speak loudly and clearly to Alexa.

Alexa is activating accidentally. How can I prevent this?

If you find Alexa is being activated accidentally you can change the wake word of your device. You can choose from either "Alexa", "Amazon" or "Echo" for the wake word.

1. In the Alexa app, select the menu icon. This looks like three horizontal lines.

2. Select "Settings"

3. Select your device

4. Select "Wake word"

5. Select your preferred wake word from the drop down menu

If you find that this issue only occurs intermittently when the environment is noisy, such as when you are hosting a party, you can temporarily mute the microphones on your device rather than changing the wake word. The mute button is located on the top of your device and resembles a microphone with a slash through it. The light ring on your device will glow red when your microphone is muted. You can press the mute button again to unmute your microphones.

How do I pair Bluetooth devices?

You can pair Bluetooth devices by doing the following:

1. Set your mobile device to Bluetooth pairing mode and ensure you are in range of your device.

2. Say, "Alexa, Pair." Alexa will notify you that your device is ready to pair.

3. Open Bluetooth settings on your mobile device and select to pair with your Amazon device. Alexa will notify you if pairing is successful.

4. If you are unable to connect, you can exit Bluetooth mode by saying "Alexa, Cancel"

5. When you wish to disconnect your mobile device you can say "Alexa, disconnect"

Once your device has been paired you will not have to repeat this process. In future when you want to connect to a previously paired device you can say "Alexa, connect."

I can't get my smart devices set up. What is wrong?

Make sure your smart device is compatible with Alexa. The list of compatible devices changes frequently, so check with Amazon if you are unsure. If your device is incompatible with Alexa, you may still by able to use it through the use of If This Then That (IFTTT). Chapter 6 of this book has details on how to use IFTTT with Alexa.

If your device is compatible with Alexa, make sure it is set up correctly on your local Wi-Fi network. You may have to download an app from your device manufacturer to get your smart device set up correctly. If you can change the name of your smart device through the manufacturers app, ensure that the name can be understood by Alexa. Stick to simple words and avoid numbers or punctuation. If you're unsure how to get your smart device set up, you should check with the device manufacturer.

If your device is set up correctly on your Wi-Fi network but you are still unable to connect, you may need to restart both your smart device and your Amazon device. Check the user manual of your smart device for instructions on how to turn it off and on again. You can also try disabling and re-enabling the skill for your device within the Alexa app. This should fix most problems.

If you have Phillips or WeMo devices, you will not need to enable a skill to discover these devices. To enable these devices, you can simply say "Alexa, discover devices".

How can I use the US/UK/Germany Alexa skills store?

To use a different version of the Alexa skills store you will need an Amazon account for that locality. You will need to reset your device and follow the instructions for setting up your device. Resetting your device will erase all of your settings and return it to the same state it was in when you first bought it.

To reset your device:

1. Use a paper clip (or similar tool) to press and hold the "**Reset**" button for five seconds. The reset button is located on the base of your device.

2. The light ring will turn orange and then blue. Wait for the light ring to turn off and then back on again. Once the light ring is glowing solid orange, your device is in setup mode.

3. You can now proceed to setup your device.

Conclusion

Thanks again for taking the time to read this book!

You should now have a good understanding of Alexa and be able to use it for a variety of different tasks!

If you enjoyed this book, please take the time to leave me a review on Amazon. I appreciate your honest feedback, and it really helps me to continue producing high quality books.